outstanding art

Lilian Coppock

Acknowledgements

The author would like to thank the children and staff of Dunbury First School for making this book possible by their enthusiasm for and commitment to Art in the curriculum. A particular debt of gratitude is due to Irene Case, Miranda Dodd and Lizi Pate.

Special thanks are also owed to Pam Wilson of Orleans Infant School for her helpful advice, and for permission to photograph her beautiful clay tile display on page 20.

Finally, a big thank you to the children of Quarleston Farm art group, especially Juliet, Jack, Jo, Pam and Beverley. It was lots of fun working with you all.

Easter frame (page 9)

Christmas frame (page 9)

First published in 1999 by Belair Publications.
Apex Business Centre, Boscombe Road, Dunstable, LU5 4RL.
Email: belair@belair-publications.co.uk

Editor: Elizabeth Miles
Design: Jane Conway
Photography: Kelvin Freeman

British Library Cataloguing in Publication Data. A catalogue record for this publication is available from the British Library.

ISBN 0 94788 230-8

The cover photograph is taken from page 58 (Edible Patchwork).

Contents

Introduction

Drawing, painting and sculptural forms have been integral to the lifestyle and beliefs of many cultures since the first cave paintings of our ancestors. Children bring a natural flair and enthusiasm to art, and three-dimensional work occupies a unique creative niche. To explore the work of sculptors, weavers and constructional artists stimulates a child's curiosity and necessitates problem-solving; it develops an awareness of texture, form, shape, space and balance; and is a pleasurable, tactile experience.

Three-dimensional work can utilise malleable materials such as clay and papier mâché, flexible materials such as wire and card, and rigid materials such as wood and plaster. Manipulating materials through constructing, moulding, carving or modelling helps to develop fine motor skills. Working with a range of materials gives valuable practice in designing, shaping and joining. Children learn to use tools safely, to co-operate with others, and to develop sensitivity to mood, movement and balance. Those who find it difficult to excel in other subjects may show great skill in three-dimensional art and design, giving them an opportunity to develop self-esteem and pride in their work.

Many curriculum subjects can be linked to three-dimensional art work. It can support topic work, such as 'Myself', 'Growing' or 'Materials'. Storybox scenes or models from stories and poetry make literacy work more exciting. Measuring or estimating proportions and considering balance and shape help to develop mathematical concepts. History and Geography come to life with masks, puppets or artefacts from other times and places. Natural collections and observations can be satisfyingly captured in clay impressions and textile interpretations. Beautiful and aesthetic tactile work can be created. Links with science and technology are particularly strong, with opportunities to explore materials and their properties, to generate designs, to visualise ideas and solve problems.

Ideas can be transferred from two-dimensional art forms to three-dimensional sculptures. For example, an outdoor sketch could be developed into a landscape painting, and then into a landscape weaving or ceramic piece. A collection of pebbles could be sketched and then modelled in clay, and painted. Drawings of trees or plants can be developed into a three-dimensional interpretation of twisted stems, using strands of wire, clay or textiles. Many items in this book can be made using materials other than those suggested.

I hope you and your children enjoy trying out the ideas in this book, developing the techniques in your own way.

Lilian Coppock

SAFETY NOTE: Some of the activities in this book will need careful supervision by a responsible adult. Always ensure the safe use of dyes, hot wax, sharp wires, saws and hammers, and glazes for clay.

Dough

Playdough

Playdough (recipe on page 71) can be modelled and repeatedly reused if it is stored in an air-tight container. Alternatively, for projects that are to be kept as a permanent record of the children's work, it can be modelled and then left to dry slowly in a warm place.

Food colouring can be mixed in with the playdough to produce an exciting range of colours. Children are particularly enthusiastic about black playdough with added glitter and sequins.

Playdough is a satisfying medium for making model cakes, dinners, animals, worms and worm holes. Try making a squeeze monster, or 'Ten fat sausages, sizzling in a pan' from *This Little Puffin* by E Matterson (Puffin, 1991). Provide simple tools such as biscuit-cutters, a garlic press for hair, grass or spaghetti, and scissors for cutting tentacles, legs or fingers.

Story Characters

Children will enjoy making a character from a favourite story, such as the character Jolly Tall shown above from *Jolly Tall* by Jane Hissey (Hutchinson, 1998).

Mix some yellow playdough and press and shape it on a board to make a giraffe. Air dry thoroughly, paint on brown spots, and then glue Jolly into a card box, decorated as shown in the story.

Names and Words

Dough letters can be made and strung together to spell words such as the children's own names. Other ideas to try could include a message for your bedroom door, a greeting in another language or the days of the week.

Shape each letter, then push a paperclip into the top of each for the string to be threaded. When completely dry decorate the letters brightly with paint, sequins and glitter, and mount on a fabric background.

Friendship Tree

Group project

This can be a group project as part of a topic on 'Myself' or can be adapted for displaying a variety of collections such as 'My family', 'Our pets', 'Our teachers' and 'People who help us at school'.

Mix a batch of playdough (recipe on page 71). Press a ball of playdough to make a face shape, and add features such as eyes, nose, ears, mouth and hair, sticking them on with water. Push in a paperclip for hanging, and thoroughly air dry before painting. Display on a cutting of tree branches.

Impressions in Playdough

All kinds of items can be pressed into dough to make impressions, ranging from the contents of a lunch box to various items in the classroom such as numbers, letters, toys and construction kit pieces. Hand and foot impressions, especially pets', are very appealing to young children.

Roll out coloured dough on paper, and press in a lightly-floured hand or foot. After air drying, outline the print with a felt-tip pen.

Note: A whole class collection of hand- or footprints is an excellent Maths resource. Use it for counting and recording the number of fingers or toes, counting in sets of five and ten, comparing and ordering sizes, and measuring and sequencing patterns of left and right prints.

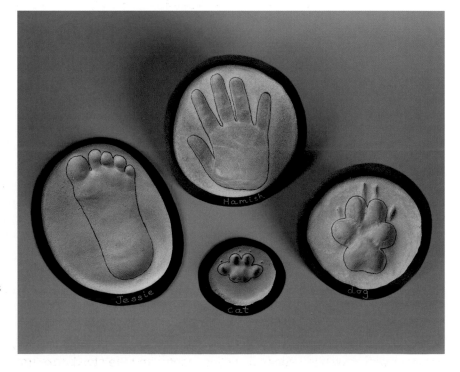

Storybox Scenes

Group project

Use a shoebox to display a scene from a favourite story. Groups of two to four children can work on a story each. Each group of children should begin by carefully planning the scene from their selected story, sketching it on paper to scale. Mix a batch of playdough (recipe on page 71). Model it to make the people, furniture and animals, joining the pieces together with water. If any models need reinforcement to make them stand up, push in a cocktail stick. Tables, beds and benches can be left to dry upside down so that they remain rigid.

Dry all the pieces thoroughly over a period of a week, turning them occasionally to ensure they dry evenly. Paint the dough pieces and decorate the inside of the shoebox using paint, papers and felt-tip pens. Assemble the scene in the shoebox and enjoy telling the story.

A class collection of scenes can be displayed by stacking the boxes on a table or stapling them to the wall, together with drawings, pieces of writing, poetry and the storybooks from which the scenes came.

Decorated Letters

Playdough letters can be decorated by pressing a range of items into the dough, without the need for glue. As well as the items mentioned below you can include a variety of painted pasta shapes, pot-pourri, shells and seaweed, or pulses and lentils.

Mix a batch of playdough (recipe on page 71). Cut out a letter from thick card, and press coloured dough onto it, smoothing it carefully with a wet finger. Neatly trim the edges.

J: Use pink playdough, with buttons and beads pressed in.

C: Use green playdough. Thread ribbons through gold-sprayed dried penne (pasta tubes) and press other ribbons into the dough at intervals with the point of a pencil. Glue on a few pearls.

P: Use yellow playdough and push in an autumn collection of cones, nuts, seeds, poppy-heads and dried flowers.

Note: Any of these ideas could be used for the picture frames on page 9. To make a Christmas wreath, shape a length of dough into a circle and press in a lavish collection of nuts, seeds, holly, cones and dried flowers. Make a hole through the dough to thread a red ribbon for hanging when the wreath is dry.

Playdough Mosaic

Collect an assortment of small items for pressing into the dough, such as dried peas and beans, beads, small pieces of coloured gravel, melon seeds and peppercorns.

Draw your mosaic design on paper, including the border. Roll out some playdough on a board, cut it to the shape you want, and very lightly mark the outline of your design on it using a pointed clay tool. Now, quite firmly, press in the mosaic items. Allow to air dry completely.

You may wish to add a little watercolour paint to the dried work, as shown right, or coloured dough may be used at the outset.

Four Seasons Picture Frames

Begin by cutting a piece of strong card 3 to 4 centimetres larger than the picture to be framed. Pencil in, on the card, the central shape of the frame (for example, oval, rectangular, wavy or zig-zag) and sketch ideas for the decorations around it.

Make batches of playdough in different colours (recipe on page 71). Add rather more food colouring than appears necessary as the colours lighten as they dry. Using the pencil line as a guide, press the coloured dough around the central shape of the card, smoothing it carefully with a wet finger. Neatly trim the edges. Model the seasonal decorations, using appropriate colours, and stick them on with water. When the frame has completely air dried, glue your chosen picture inside. Repeat the process to make a suitable frame for each season.

Note: As the finish is a soft pastel colour you may wish to brighten or darken some details with paint or touches of felt-tip pen. If you need just a tiny quantity of one colour, knead a little food colouring directly into a small piece of uncoloured dough instead of adding the colour to the mixing water.

Salt Dough

To make salt dough follow the recipe on page 71. Salt dough keeps well if it is stored in a plastic bag in a fridge. The texture improves over time. If it gets too soft knead in a little flour.

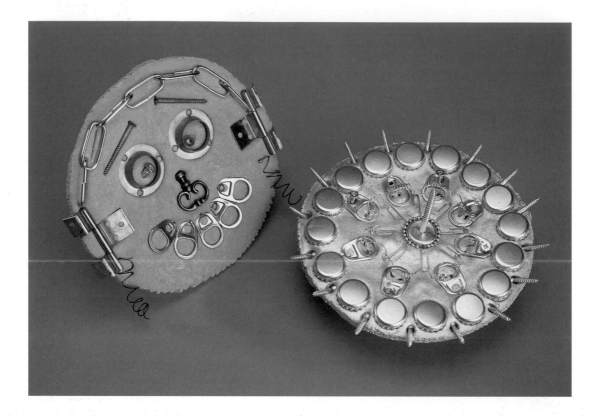

Metal Collage

To make a metal collage, first collect an interesting assortment of metal oddments such as bottletops, nuts, chains, ring-pulls, screws, paperclips, springs, hinges, keys, pins, washers and wire.

Make some salt dough and roll it out on an oiled baking tray until 1 centimetre thick. Cut the dough to shape and firmly push in the metal pieces. Their arrangement can be planned on paper first to avoid making unnecessary impressions in the dough. Bake (see page 71) and spray or paint, as desired.

Tutankhamun

Roll out a large piece of salt dough on a greased baking tray. Shape and add pieces of dough for the eyes, nose, mouth and beard, sticking them on with water. Indent further detail with clay tools.

When the model is baked and cooled, spray it all over with gold paint, dry it off and add turquoise highlights with poster paint. Finally, glue the model onto stiff card with PVA glue and decorate the edges of the card with gold-sprayed pasta shells and glitter glue.

Food Modelling

Christmas Dinner

Make up a batch of salt dough (recipe on page 71). To create the dinner service press salt dough over an oiled plate and bowl, and trim the edges. Model a selection of food items: roast turkey with all the trimmings, and Christmas pudding and custard are shown above. Stick the food onto the dishes using water to bind them. Make cutlery by pressing plastic cutlery into dough and cutting around it. When the dough is baked hard, paint the contents of the dinner in appropriate colours and spray the cutlery silver. Display as a complete meal with place settings and accessories.

My Lunch Box

Use salt dough to model a selection of favourite lunch box items such as fruit, sandwiches, juice, nuts and biscuits. Bake and paint. Make a lunch box from two tissue boxes, and put the lunch items inside.

Worms in Emmenthal

Cut a wedge of 'cheese' from salt dough and poke holes into it with fingers and pencils. Use water to stick little dough worms into some of the holes. Bake and paint.

Story Slab

Group project

Make up a batch of salt dough (recipe on page 71) and oil a large baking sheet. Sketch out a design from a chosen story – Winnie the Pooh and friends are shown above. A few children could make the tree and grassy base first, directly onto the baking tray. Each child can then make one or more of the characters and stick them on with water. Bake and paint the completed scene. Paint some stiff card an appropriate background colour and mount the slab onto it. Allow the slab to dry off completely before sticking it onto the card with PVA glue.

Pictures in Frames

With Cellophane glued to the back, these look very pretty against a window.

First, draw a simple outline picture of, for example, a cat or a tree, onto a piece of greaseproof paper. Draw a frame round it, ensuring that the picture touches the frame at several points. Press rolls or pieces of salt dough over the paper pattern, using water to join overlapping pieces. Bake until hard, remove the greaseproof paper and paint. Finally, stick Cellophane onto the back of the frame with masking tape.

Note: If you wish to hang up your frame, before baking either push in a paperclip at the top or make a hole through the dough. After baking thread ribbon through the hole.

Salt Dough over Wire

Older children will enjoy the challenge of making a 'holes sculpture' using salt dough pressed around a wire armature (a wire frame on which to mould a sculpture).

To make the armature you need three 30-centimetre-long strips of florist's wire. Put them together and twist them firmly in two places – a third and two-thirds of the way along. Stand the wires upright, spreading out the wires at the base to make the armature stable and balanced. Working from the bottom to the top, cover the wire with salt dough, squeezing and smoothing the dough into shape. Make lots of dough tendrils using a garlic press, dip them in water and drape them over the sculpture.

After it has been baked and cooled, the sculpture can be painted, sprayed or decorated in any way you wish.

People Frames

The central space in one of these frames can be used to display a photograph, drawing, or piece of stitching, as shown.

Oil a medium-sized baking tray, and use pieces of salt dough to build a person. Leave the body open in the centre to make the frame. This can be in any shape you choose, such as circular, square or heart-shaped. Make the figure amusing by adding lots of detail such as garlic-pressed hair, knobbly knees, fingers and facial details.

When baked and cooled, paint the figure with watercolour paints. Place the item chosen for display in the frame and add a loop of wire for hanging.

13

Clay

Simple Shapes and Impressions

Children need lots of practice handling clay. By rolling, pressing, stretching, squeezing and smoothing it they will discover its unique properties and gain valuable experience in basic skills.

Beads: Roll terracotta clay into balls or cylinders. Use a stick to make a hole through each ball and to scratch patterns on the surfaces of the 'beads'. Once dry, fire and string together.

Horseshoe: Look at a real horseshoe and discuss how it was made. Roll out a sausage of clay, then curve and flatten it. Impress it with nails and push in a paperclip for hanging. When completely dry burnish it with black shoe polish. Try making life-size shoes for a shire horse, pony or donkey.

Heart: Use a biscuit-cutter to cut a heart shape from a rolled slab of clay. Decorate the heart with a flower pattern and push a paperclip into the top for hanging. When dry, apply a mixture of paint and glitter.

Thumb pot: Roll some clay into a ball approximately 5 centimetres in diameter. Smooth its surface, then push in a thumb. Keep turning and pressing the clay until it is a good shape. Flatten the base gently and scratch a pattern around the pot. When dry, coat with diluted PVA glue to create a good shine.

Slabs: Roll out the clay with a rolling pin so that it is 1 centimetre thick. If rolled onto a piece of hessian it will be easier to lift. Cut out a circle shape using a round template, and make impressions with an interesting selection of round items such as cogs, wheels, rings, screws, springs, construction kit bricks or poppy-heads. Try to arrange the items to represent a machine or engine as shown right. Push a paperclip into the side for hanging, dry completely and spray with gold or silver paint. Slabs can be cut into oval shapes to make eggs for Easter.

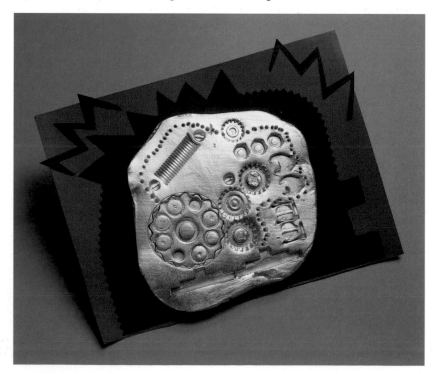

Note: Use clay impressions as part of topic work. For example, for an autumn theme try rolling items such as leaves, ferns, pine needles, wheat, lime seeds, poppy-heads or Michaelmas daisies into the clay.

Balls of Clay

Candleholders

These all begin as a ball of clay, with handles or bases attached with slip (see page 71).

Rounded candleholder: To make a sea anemone shape, flatten a ball of clay and scrape grooves down the sides with the fingers. Add pattern details if desired.

Cube candleholder: Flatten a ball of clay on all sides by banging it on a flat worktop.

Diwa lamp and round pots: Begin with a basic thumb-pot shape made from a ball of clay. Add handles or bases, if desired. (Diwa lamps are made to celebrate the Hindu festival of Diwali.)

To make the holes for the candles, choose a candle or night light and push it firmly into the candleholder you have made. Make the hole a little wider than the candle as the clay will shrink as it dries.

Note on finishing: Completed pieces may be painted when dry, or fired and glazed if you have access to a kiln. Remember that if solid shapes are fired there will be breakages, so while the clay is still soft make a hole right through the ball or cube, or wait until the clay is leather-hard and scoop out the underside to make it concave.

Cut Fruit

Each item begins as a clay ball, which is then dropped onto a worktop to flatten it on one side. Pinch out a stalk, or if you need to add a pointed or rounded end squeeze the hemisphere gently. Study the seed patterns in real fruits before scratching out a pattern of seeds on the flat face of the clay model. When the clay is quite dry, paint on a layer of white powder paint, followed by soft watercolours. These can be blended to match the real fruit.

Note: 'Fruit slices' also make good subjects for slab work.

15

Relief Slabs

Plaques

Slabs are easy to make and adaptable to any topic work.

Show the children how to roll out the clay to an even thickness by rolling it between two long strips of wood, 1 centimetre square. Roll the slab on a piece of hessian, so that it does not stick and can be easily lifted.

Cut out your chosen shape for the plaque from the rolled slab. Model pieces of clay into letters, flower petals, fish, facial features or trees, and attach these to the slab with slip (see page 71). Impress other details with a pointed clay tool. Try adding a twisted worm border or use clay pushed through a garlic press to produce textured hair, pond weed or flower centres. Make one or two holes through the slab so that the plaque can be hung. When completely dry, the slab can be painted or sprayed.

Masks

These are African-inspired masks, but the idea could be used for any other culture. Begin by looking at reference books and sketching out ideas on paper before working in clay.

Roll out a slab of clay, 1.5 centimetres thick, on hessian and cut out an oval shape. Cut away clay to make holes for the eyes and mouth, and attach prominent features such as the nose, lips, hair and horns with slip. Use clay tools to draw patterns in the clay, and drape the completed mask over a ball of newspaper or plate to dry. This will give it a convex shape. Fire when completely dry.

Heads

The heads, shown left, are made from a ball or a slab of clay.

Head in a hat: Begin with a ball of clay and make a large finger hole in the base so that it can be fired. Add details with clay tools and attach feet, nose and hat with slip.

Head with a tongue: Make a thumb pot (see page 14 for information on how to make a thumb pot). Turn it upside down and add tongue and nose details with slip.

Round head: Push a broom handle into a ball of clay. Smooth the clay down and around the handle to form a thick neck, then remove the handle. Ensure the base stands level. Mould and shape facial details.

Profile head: Roll a slab of clay 2 centimetres thick. Cut the chosen shape out with a clay tool or scissors. Cut out and engrave further detail. Flatten the base so that it will stand up.

Clay Characters

Clay may be used in a variety of ways when making people.

King finger puppet: Glue a clay head to a card-cone body (or use a yoghurt pot or strip of fabric). Push a pencil hole in the wet clay, big enough for a finger.

Seated figure: Little Miss Muffet can be cut out with scissors from a 1.5-centimetre-thick slab of clay. Sit the figure firmly on a lid or ball of clay, and arrange the arms and legs.

Standing figure: Roll out a thick tube of clay. Squeeze it at the neck and flatten it at the base. Carefully placed impressions on the face and the arrangement of the arms can successfully convey feelings of surprise (as shown), fear, joy, sadness or anger.

Animal Shapes

Children enjoy modelling animals that are linked to familiar themes and stories. Each animal, shown left, is an example of a different technique.

Owl (slab): Roll out a 1.5-centimetre-thick slab of clay. Cut out the animal shape, scratch out the details and curve the base to make it stand up.

Cat (thumb pot): Make a shallow thumb pot from a ball of clay (see page 14). Model a head and tail from oddments of clay, and attach them to the front and back of the pot, using slip.

Tiger (tube): Roll a tube of clay and pinch out the head and legs. Attach other features, such as a tail and ears, with slip (see page 71). Try making a caterpillar, teddy, insect or farm animal, in the same way.

Bird (ball): Roll out a ball of clay and pinch out features such as a beak and tail. Feathers, sticks and seeds can be pushed in for extra details. Try making a hedgehog, frog, fish or hippo.

Note: When the animals have been completed, they can be finished in a variety of ways. The bird is terracotta clay glossed with diluted PVA glue. The owl is burnished with shoe polish and a soft brush. The tiger (which needs to be hollowed out underneath) and the cat were both fired, then the tiger was painted with acrylic paints and the cat was glazed.

Butterfly Life Cycle

Press a fresh leaf, veins down, into a 1.5-centimetre-thick clay slab by rolling it with a rolling pin. Cut out four leaf impressions. Model each stage of the butterfly's life cycle in clay (egg, caterpillar, pupa and adult) and attach them to the leaves with slip. Allow the leaves to dry on crumpled newspaper to create a natural, curled look. Finish by painting with watercolours.

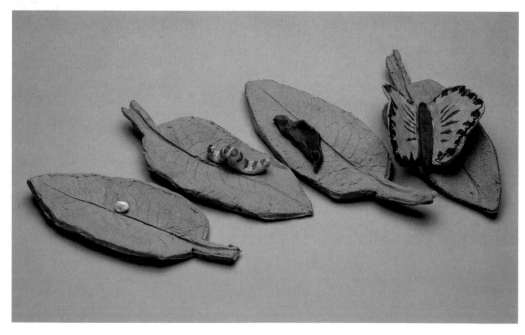

Joining Two Clay Slabs

Thatched Cottage

Begin by sketching a thatched cottage and garden from a photograph or in situ if possible.

Roll out two slabs of clay about 1.5 centimetres thick and cut out the shapes of the house and the garden. Make sure there is a straight edge at the bottom of the house.

Use clay tools, a toothbrush and garlic press to add the windows, door, brickwork, flint, thatch, hedge, path and plants. You might also attach a cat or a person working in the garden, with slip (see page 71).

Let the two slabs dry off for a few hours before joining them. Score and add slip to the back edge of the garden and the bottom edge of the house. Carefully press the two slabs together so that they are at right angles. An extra roll of clay can be attached at the back for additional strength. Dry off completely, and fire if possible.

Note: 'My house' is an excellent topic for clay-slab work. Even the youngest children can scratch out a simple house design on a flat clay slab.

Joining Two Thumb Pots

This kind of hollow shape could be used for a variety of amusing heads, or for the bodies of a range of animals and birds.

Make two thumb pots of the same size (see page 14). Score the top edges, paint on slip and press them gently together. Smooth the join carefully. Model small pieces of clay into legs, ears, a trunk, snout and so on, and attach them with slip to create different clay animal characters.

Note: Remember that when firing hollow clay shapes it is essential to make a hole through the clay so that air can escape. The elephant has a top slit, turning it into a money box, and the pig has eye holes that pass right through the clay.

Tile Display Board

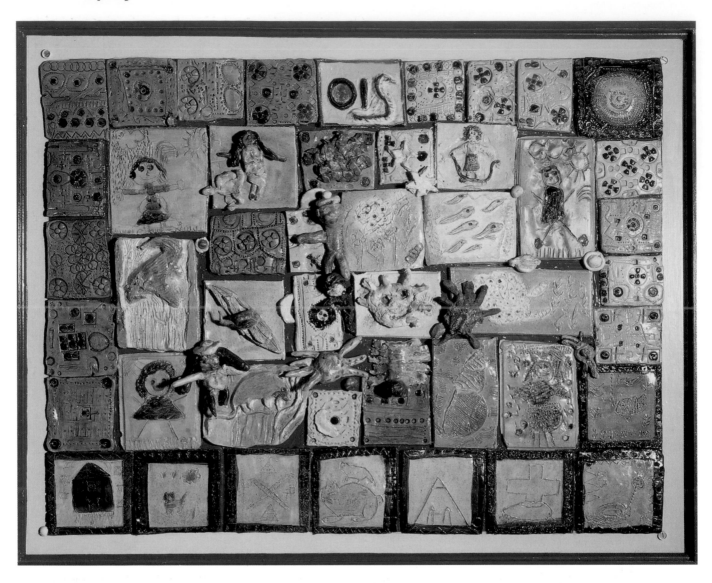

A mixed collection of clay slabs and models can be assembled on a large piece of marine board to make a stimulating and tactile display, as well as a welcoming feature at the school entrance.

Roll out 1-centimetre-thick slabs of clay in an assortment of sizes, from 10 x 10 centimetres up to 10 x 20 centimetres. Use clay tools to etch patterns and drawings into the slabs or to make impressions in them. Alternatively, add pieces of clay that have been shaped into figures or animals and attach them firmly with slip (see page 71). A mixture of techniques – etching, impressing and adding clay – works well. Model separate little figures of people, minibeasts or animals. Arrange them on the tiles so that they overlap some of the spaces between the tiles. The slabs and models could be based on a single theme, such as pets, houses, the school pond, playground games, or a visit to the airport (seaside, farm, zoo or river).

Fire the work when it is completely dry, and then glaze and fire it again. A variety of commercial glazes may be mixed to produce additional colours. Interesting and unexpected colour blends may result where colours overlap. Some tiles could have shiny glaze, some matt, some speckled. Glaze must not be painted on the back or the edges of tiles – use a damp sponge to wipe off drips. Use the correct pottery brush, if possible.

Some of the tiles above had tiny chips of blue and green glass added to the second firing. This melts into the depressions on firing, creating a beautiful effect.

Note: Careful supervision is required when glazing – some glazes can be poisonous.

Coil Pots

People Pots

Cover a small flowerpot with cling film to use as a mould and to give an even shape. Roll and cut a round slab of clay to fit the base, and stand the pot on it. Then roll sausages of clay approximately 1 centimetre in width. Wind these around the pot, coiling them up from the base, until the flowerpot is nearly covered. Join the coils with a little slip as you work (see page 71).

The outside may be

- left as coils

- completely smoothed with a spatula and damp sponge

- patterned by gently pushing the coils into each other with a rounded stick.

Leave for a few hours until the clay has dried off a little and then remove the flowerpot. Smooth the inside of the clay with a wet finger or lollystick, pushing the coils firmly together. Finally, make a stick person from coils of clay, add wild hair (clay pushed through a garlic press) and attach it to the pot with slip. Dry off completely, then fire or paint.

Large Spring Pot

Roll out a 1.5-centimetre-thick slab of clay on hessian, and cut out a circle for the base of the pot. Roll out 1.5-centimetre-thick sausages of clay and begin to coil them around the edge of the base, joining each with slip. After adding four or five coils, smooth both the inside and outside of the pot with a spatula, and tape a strip of card or rolled newspaper round the pot, to stop it sagging. Add more coils until your pot is tall enough and then smooth it inside and out. Allow the pot to dry off overnight, ensuring that the shape is well-supported with taped, card strips or newspaper.

The following day remove the wrappings and decorate the pot. Model little chicks, eggs, blossom, daffodils and butterflies out of clay, and attach them around the pot with slip. Fire the pot, if possible, or add shine with diluted PVA glue.

Note: A 'topic pot' is fun to make. For example, a theme on 'Ancient Greece' could have heroes, monsters and gods attached to the pot while a 'Pets' theme could have modelled pets, with their food and cages.

Fired Glazed Tiles

To make the animal tiles shown above roll out 1-centimetre-thick slabs of clay and cut them into 10-centimetre squares. Draw the design onto a tile with a pointed clay tool, and add a border pattern if desired. Allow the tile to dry off, then fire it in a kiln.

Provide the children with a selection of five or six coloured glazes to paint onto their work. Remember to keep the back and sides of the slab free of glaze. Fire again.

Note: Careful supervision is required when glazing – some glazes can be poisonous.

Fired Painted Tiles

To make a Greek legend tile (Medusa is shown right) roll out a slab of clay 1 centimetre thick, and cut out a square. Build up the picture with pieces of clay attached with slip (see page 71), and incise other lines or patterns. Dry off and fire.

Using small brushes, paint the tile with a selection of bright acrylic paints. Acrylics dry quickly and give a pleasant gloss to the work.

Note: Remember to wash all brushes and pots in hot water before the paint dries.

Advanced Slab Project

'My front door' is a challenging project for older children as it requires careful planning and measuring skills. Ask the children to take photographs or make detailed sketches of both the inside and outside of their own front door.

Use squared paper to draw a pattern of 'My front door'. Draw the pattern to scale as shown in the illustration. Cut out the five basic pieces you will need: one door, one top, one base and two sides. Roll and cut out five slabs of clay, using the paper patterns as a guide. Make the base slab at least 1.5 centimetres thick. A bowharp is useful for cutting slabs of even thickness.

Let the slabs dry off for an hour or so until the clay can be handled without collapsing. During this time additional details can be modelled, such as a doormat, boots or umbrella.

Assemble the pieces by first attaching the door centrally onto the base with slip (see page 71). Then add the sides and the top, ensuring all joins are scored and painted with slip. Scratch in the details of tiles, door, letterbox or glass, and attach any other additional clay details with slip.

Allow to dry off completely, supporting the work with boxes if necessary. Fire and glaze, or paint with acrylics.

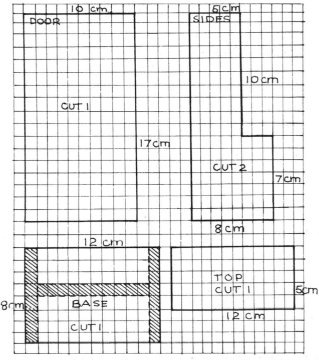

Pattern for 'My Front Door'

Papier Mâché

Layering Paper over a Mould

Layering paper over a mould gives a smoother finish than using moulded paper pulp (see page 28). Paste overlapping pieces of torn paper, about 3 x 4 centimetres, over the chosen mould, which should be covered with cling film or petroleum jelly for easy release. The first layer of paper should be wetted, not pasted. (A useful tip: when building up several layers use alternate layers of different coloured papers such as white and yellow newsprint to ensure consistent coverage and that no areas are missed.) A range of different paper can be used, and beautiful effects can be created with coloured sugar paper, tissue paper or wrapping paper. Use cellulose paste that is non-fungicidal and suitable for children. Diluted PVA glue may be used instead – this requires fewer layers and dries more quickly. The work needs to be dried completely in a warm place, before easing it off the mould and decorating.

Cup and saucer: Apply six layers of wrapping paper over a saucer and inside a cup. Use a little roll of pasted paper to make the handle.

Pink bowl: Apply four layers of sugar paper inside a bowl, alternating layers of light and dark pink. The colours will run together, producing an interesting effect.

Basket: Apply six alternating layers of blue and white tissue paper over a large yoghurt pot. Add a twisted tissue handle, dried over a bottle, and flecks of blue tissue.

Sports Day cup: Cover two differently shaped bowls using five layers of newspaper for each. Glue the two bases together when they are dry and spray with silver paint. Decorate with ribbon.

Tall pot: Apply five layers of newspaper over a plastic pot. When dry, decorate with string and dried peas. Spray with gold paint and add bits of coloured foil.

Star plate: Apply four layers of copier paper over a large plate (white paper gives a better surface for painting than newsprint). Make a star template and draw round it on the plate mould. Cut the plate mould into a star shape, sponge paint it with dark blue and black, add stick-on stars and decorate with a gold marker pen. All kinds of other finishes could be applied, such as marbling, potato printing or splash-and-drip painting.

Layering over a Balloon

Animals

Blow up balloons to about 12 centimetres in diameter, tie securely and apply four layers of newspaper pieces (as on page 21). Support each balloon on a flowerpot, turning it as you work. When covered, hang the balloon up to dry for a few days.

Now design your bird or animal shape – a fish, owl, rabbit, lion, hedgehog or any of the animals shown right. Tape on tubes for legs and card pieces for the ears, trunk, wings or tail. Eggbox sections can be used to make snouts, bulging eyes, udders or short legs. Glue card feet to the base of any shape that might roll over. Paste a final layer of newsprint over the shape, covering all the joins well.

When the paste is dry, pop the balloon, then remove it and paste paper over the hole. Finish the animal by painting or by gluing on wrapping paper, tissue paper, wool, feathers or sawdust.

Piñata

Group project

The piñata is a Mexican birthday tradition – a clay ball filled with sweets, tiny presents, flowers and toys is hung on a pole. Children take turns to be blindfolded and try to smash open the piñata with a stick.

To make a papier-mâché piñata use a basic hollow balloon shape, as for the animals above. The piñata could be a bird, animal, face or fantasy creature. A star shape is made by taping on five card cones. Paint and decorate lavishly when it is dry, fill with treats and hang it on a pole.

25

Musical Paper Layering

Maracas

Blow up two balloons to 13 centimetres in diameter, and begin layering paper over them (as on page 25). Cover with four layers of newspaper pieces and one layer of brightly coloured wrapping paper pieces, such as the animal print shown.

When the paste is completely dry, pop the balloon, remove it and insert a few dried beans, pulses or rice. Push a piece of glued broom handle into the hole and decorate the handle. A coat of diluted PVA glue will strengthen the finished surface.

Fruit and Vegetable Shakers

Any firm fruit or vegetable can be used as a mould. Grease it lightly and apply five layers of newspaper pieces. When the paste is dry, an adult can cut the mould in half with a craft knife and remove the fruit. Insert either a bell, some buttons, nails, paperclips or macaroni into each fruit. Paste the two halves of the fruit together with pieces of white paper to give a good surface for painting with watercolours.

Note: A slice of watermelon is too wet to use as a mould. To make the one shown right use a card armature made from a folded circle of card loosely taped around the curve. Cover this with three layers of newsprint and one of white paper. Leave a small hole at the corner for inserting peas as the slice does not need to be cut in half.

Layered Head for a Baby

This life-size baby's head can be made by covering an inflated balloon with five layers of newspaper pieces (see page 25). Make the baby's features from paper pulp (see page 71) glued on with PVA and make the neck from a yoghurt pot taped and pasted into place. Cover the whole head with a layer of white kitchen paper to provide a good surface for painting.

When the head is completely dry, remove the balloon, cover the hole with paper, and paint the head. Paint on a layer of diluted PVA glue for strength. Apply PVA glue round the neck and stick it inside a baby suit stuffed with kapok. Glue card hands inside the cuffs.

This makes an amusing addition to the home corner, hospital or baby clinic.

Masks and Profiles

Make up a batch of newspaper pulp (see page 71).

Masks: On a paper plate, mark and cut out the eye holes. Then add facial features, such as hair and eyebrows, by gently pressing and shaping small pieces of paper pulp to the plate.

Profiles: Draw the profile of a head on thick card and fill in the outline with paper pulp. Add raised parts for lips, eyebrows and ears, and a depression for the eye.

Leave the pulp modelling to dry in a warm place for at least a week before painting, decorating, adding collage or taping a stick to the masks.

Paper Pulp over a Mould

Pots and bowls made with paper pulp are more textured and quicker to make than layered pots, but they take longer to dry because the paper is thicker. Pulp pots can be quite strong, especially if other materials are added.

The papers used can vary from the grey of pulped newsprint to the soft brown of parcel paper, or from the pastels of sugar paper to the vivid colours of paper napkins. Any papers may be pulped – poster paper, wrapping paper, tissue paper, speckled envelopes, paper bags or computer paper – and each will produce quite different results. Gorgeous effects can be created by mixing flower petals, seeds, sequins or glittering threads into the pulp.

Mix the pulp by soaking, liquidising, sieving and adding paste to your chosen paper (see page 71). Mix in any colour or added items you wish. Cover your mould with cling film and apply a 1-centimetre-thick layer of pulp. Younger children find it easier to press pulp into a shallow mould than around a tall mould. Allow to dry completely in a warm place before removing the mould. A rustic, natural edging adds to the charm.

Red bowl: Pulp red paper napkins. Add sequins and glitter.

Blue bowl: Pulp blue poster paper. Add glittery threads.

Brown pot: Pulp brown wrapping paper. Add sawdust and an etched pattern.

Blue plate: Use newspaper pulp. Add melon seeds, blue wool and blue food colouring.

Pink bowl: Pulp eggboxes and add pot-pourri.

Purple bowl: Use two sugar-paper pulps (pink and purple).

Note: Experiment with colour and texture. Try adding paint, coffee, turmeric, snips of ribbon or foils, tiny beads, rosemary leaves or dried flowers. Think of other items you could add.

Modelling with Coloured Pulp

Posy of Scented Flowers

Mix up several different colours of paper pulp, using brightly coloured papers (see page 71).

Cut some stems from card, or use hay stalks or twigs, and lay them on a plastic bag over a board. Next, using paper pulp, mould a flower over the end of each stem. Make the petals first, and then use a contrasting colour for the centre. Press a little lavender into the centre for fragrance (or add a few drops of rosewater when the flowers are dry). When completely dried, tie three flowers into a posy using a paper doily and ribbon.

Butterfly Mobile

These require a range of different coloured paper pulps. Put each one in a separate container (the pulps will keep well if the containers are air-tight).

Look carefully at pictures of butterflies and draw an outline on a piece of thin, clear plastic. Fill in the outline with paper pulp, keeping it as symmetrical as possible. Add tiny pieces of pulp in one or two contrasting colours to make patterns.

Position a half-opened paperclip centrally, and roll a sausage of black pulp for the body. Press the black pulp down the centre of the butterfly over the paperclip, so that a small loop stands up for attaching a string. Push in some bent wire for antennae and dry completely before hanging.

Bowl Landscapes

Inverted bowl shapes can become very imaginative scenes. Use a curved bowl as a mould, cover with cling film and press in a 1-centimetre layer of paper pulp (see page 28). Allow to dry completely before creating your scene.

Desert island: Use yellow pulp for the island and blue for the sea around it. While this is still wet, push in some sticks for palm trees and a few tiny stones and shells. When completely dry, decorate with tissue-paper vegetation, a paper castaway, wild animals, and sharks in the sea.

Moonscape: Make this with newspaper pulp. When the bowl is dry, spray with silver paint for an interesting, rough, moon-like texture. Attach eggbox sections and circular lids covered with foil. Add an astronaut or lunar module to the moonscape.

Bowl Gardens

Colour newspaper pulp with food colouring or paint, and press it into a bowl lined with cling film to make a garden for families of minibeasts, such as mice, spiders, turtles, frogs or ladybirds. Make the family of minibeasts from little hemispheres of coloured pulp. Allow the bowl and insects to dry completely.

Decorate the bowl garden with glued-on papers, gravel, moss, bark, pot-pourri or anything else you wish. Glue card legs onto the insects, and introduce them to their new home!

Note: To avoid making a papier-mâché bowl you can cheat by substituting it with a bought one (used for hanging baskets).

Layering over Armatures

Bottle Cats

Choose strong plastic bottles of different shapes and sizes. Cover with two pasted layers of overlapping newspaper pieces. Squeeze pasted paper into cone shapes for ears, and a long strip for a tail, and glue into place. Cover with a final layer of white kitchen paper. When the cats are dry, paint them brightly to give each cat its own character.

Note: Bottle shapes also make excellent people.

Lady with Dog

Group project

The children can work in groups to design an animal or child-size person that is free-standing. Make the armatures from cardboard cartons and tubes, arranged and glued together to give the basic shape. Cover with three layers of pasted brown paper strips. When the model is completely dry, cut up white or black paper to make fine details such as hair, clothes and facial features, and glue them in place.

31

Landscape over an Armature

A variety of landscapes can be made to support work in Science or Geography, such as an island, desert or polar scene, a lunar or volcanic landscape, or a swamp habitat. The stimulus for the hill landscape shown above was 'Animals that live in holes'.

Use a strong piece of card or hardboard for the base of the landscape. Decide where hills, river valleys or seas will go and draw them on the base. Build up the high areas with boxes, pieces of foam or plastic waste, glued into place. Tape balls of newspaper to fill in holes and soften hard edges. Tape in small plastic flowerpots or pieces of plastic pipe for holes and caves (as shown in the photograph above).

When you are satisfied with the overall shape, cover the whole landscape with pasted strips of newspaper, about 4 x 20 centimetres in size. Build up three layers of overlapping strips and add a final layer of strong sugar paper torn into rough strips, smoothing and contouring the hills, caves and valleys with the fingers.

Allow the landscape to dry completely, then paint and collage it with twigs, pebbles, sand, bark, foils and papers. Finally, add the movable items such as dinosaurs, astronauts, swamp monsters, pirates and so on. Make the animals for the 'holes' landscape (badger, fox, mouse, vole, rabbit, shrew, mole and worms) with moulded newspaper pulp, dried and painted (see page 71).

Note: Completed landscapes are an exciting stimulus for small-world imaginative play and for creative writing. The children can imagine they are in the landscape and describe what they see and feel and what might happen next.

Wire and String

Wire Figures

Wire and Polystyrene

To make these amusing skeletons you will need five 30-centimetre-long pieces of florist's wire, and an assortment of white polystyrene shapes such as tiles, trays and other packaging.

Begin by cutting a skull shape from polystyrene and gluing on paper scraps for features. Push a piece of wire through the skull, and make a loop at the top for hanging. Twist two more pieces of wire together for the arms and wind these firmly under the skull. Now thread polystyrene 'bones' onto the arms and spine. Finally, twist two more pieces of wire together for the legs, attach them firmly at the base of the spine and thread on leg 'bones'. Arrange the limbs at interesting angles for the best effect, and hang as a mobile or set into a tray of plaster as a free-standing figure.

Wire and Aluminium Foil

Make these figures for a topic on sport or health from four pieces of florist's wire and aluminium foil.

Begin by pressing two small balls of Plasticine onto the work surface for the feet. Push a piece of wire into each Plasticine ball and twist the two wires firmly together at the top (for the neck) and again, lower down, to make a body shape. Bend a third piece of wire into a loop for the head, and attach it securely to the neck. Wind a fourth piece of wire around the neck a few times to make the arms.

Now dress the figure by crushing pieces of aluminium foil over the wire to cover the head, body and limbs. Add any additional details in coloured foils, and pose your figure as a dancer, tennis player, footballer or athlete.

Note: Try animals made of wire, with foil crumpled over.

33

Wire and String in Plaster Slabs

Collect a good assortment of coloured wire pieces and springs, together with oddments of rope, string, pipe-cleaners, gravel and bits of wood. Show the children some of the ways in which wire can be used, for example, how to curl it into a spiral, zig-zag it, coil it around a pencil and how to cut it.

The children can then make their picture to fit in their chosen container (a plastic dish, polystyrene tray or cardboard lid). When the children are happy with their picture design, remove it from the container and carefully arrange it alongside the container on the work surface.

Now mix the plaster, following the instructions on page 71. Pour plaster into the container to a depth of about 1 centimetre and level it, tapping the container gently to remove air bubbles. When it is just on the point of setting, quickly and lightly arrange the wire, string, rope and stones onto it, so that they are only just embedded in the plaster.

Leave the picture to set in the dish for several hours before carefully turning it out. Add sponge printing or any other painted details when the plaster has completely dried. Glue the picture to stiff card for extra strength.

Note: Household finishing plaster makes a cheap and acceptable substitute for plaster of Paris.

Wool and String Wrapping

Wrapped Tubes

Standing figures can be made by wrapping coloured yarns round card tubes or plastic containers.

Show the children how to wind the yarn round a tube, keeping the strands close together and not too loose. The ends can be taped down or held down under a few rounds of yarn. Tuck the final end securely into the work.

For the tube figures, glue on a paper face and wrapped oddments of card for the arms. Finish with a tuft of unravelled string for the hair.

Wrapped Landscape

Select a variety of coloured yarns for skies, hills and fields, such as seasonal colours for autumn or winter, or regional colours for desert or savannah landscapes.

On a piece of strong card, draw straight and sloping pencil lines to show where the bands of colour should be. Tape down an end of 'sky' yarn on the top back corner of the card, and start winding the yarn round the card, following the pencil lines. Try to obtain a pleasing mix of colours and textures in the choice of yarns. Colours can be wrapped over others, or just one wrap could be added here and there to add detail. Tape all loose ends to the back of the card. Glue on a tree or other feature made from an oddment of unravelled rope.

Note: Try wrapping initial letters, picture frames or Valentine frames, all cut from card.

String Design

Collect an assortment of different types of string in natural or dyed colours, such as hemp, sisal, jute, nylon, cotton, gardening string, curtain cords, pieces of rope and fishing net. Each type has its individual way of curling, springing and separating:

Sisal (such as packing string) is stiff, springy and unravels easily into separate strands.

Jute (such as sack cloth) is softer, unravels into knotty loops and untidy webs.

Hemp (such as plumber's tow) is silky, soft and fluffy when unravelled.

Cotton (such as dishcloth yarn) is soft, loops easily and unravels into neat ends.

Nylon is strong, shiny and unravels into interesting tangles.

String can be used straight, unwound, chopped into small pieces, tied in knots or bows, plaited, looped, woven, curled or unravelled.

Ways in which to begin

- Experiment with patterns such as spirals, loops, circles, crosses, rows of short pieces or chequerboard. Try tying a knot in a 5-centimetre length and unravel both ends.

- On a board, stick down a curling length of string as a series of loops. Fill in the loops and spaces with a string pattern.

- Stick down several long pieces of string all in the same direction such as top to bottom. Fill in the spaces between with patterns.

- Sketch an idea from the natural world such as tree bark, seed heads or feathers. Glue string outlines and patterns over the sketch.

- Sketch an animal outline such as the owl and horse shown above. Glue thick string over the outline and fill in with patterns.

Note: Always use PVA glue. Thick rope may need weighting down until the glue sets. Additional materials may be glued on to develop a pattern, such as buttons, dried beans, pasta, lace or foils.

Wire Outlines

Valentine Hearts

To make the frame cut a long strip of lacy net curtain about 65 x 3 centimetres in size. Then thread a 50-centimetre length of bendy rod wire in and out of the holes in the lace and twist the two ends together. Bend the wire and lace into a heart shape.

Design an inside for the frame using red card, foils and wire or ribbon. Draw and cut out an arrow from card, and glue it to the frame. Pierce a hole with a needle into tiny card hearts, push wire through and twist securely. Make wire coils by wrapping wire round a pencil. Attach all the heart messages and coils securely to the frame and hang up the finished work with a red ribbon.

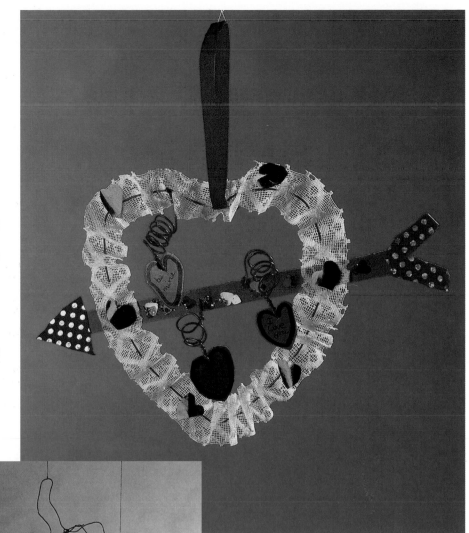

Faces

You will need some bendy wire, such as florist's wire or plastic-coated wire, and wire cutters.

Make the frame of the face first by bending and joining the wire into an oval shape. Show the children how to twist the ends firmly together.

Add pieces of wire inside the oval frame for the eyes, nose and mouth, bending and joining carefully where necessary. The children will invent all kinds of ways to attach the nose. Create small details, such as nostrils, pupils or eyebrows, with short lengths of wire. Finish off with ears and hair, or a hat.

Giant Outdoor Flowers

These colourful plastic flowers are fun to make and can be 'planted' in the school garden for the Summer term.

You will need an assortment of colourful plastic bags, bamboo canes, florist's wire to give rigidity to the plastic and some stiff plastic mesh.

For the five petals, cut five circles about 20 centimetres in diameter from a plastic bag. Thread a piece of florist's wire in and out across each petal, and bend over the outer ends of the wire, so that the plastic will not slip off. Collect up the five inner ends of wire centrally and twist them firmly together. Staple the petals together where they overlap, to strengthen the shape.

For the flower centre, cut a circular piece of stiff plastic mesh and join it to the petals by pushing the wire ends through the mesh and twisting the ends around at random. Now decorate the mesh brightly with oddments of plastic strips, Cellophane and foils – try weaving, tying, plaiting and stapling. The children will be very imaginative. Add any other decoration you wish to the flower, stapling everything securely together.

Finally, tie the flower to a piece of bamboo cane with some firmly twisted wire. Add a few green plastic leaves and then 'plant' your flower.

Advanced Wire Projects

Winter Tree

Push ten pieces of florist's wire, 30 centimetres long, into a flattened ball of clay. Each of these will become a branch of the tree, so spread them out at the top into a tree shape.

Wind more pieces of wire around the trunk and out on to each branch, making loops, coils and bends. Continue winding and pressing until each branch is roughly wrapped in wire.

Keep the tree centrally balanced so that it will not topple, bending branches into shape if necessary. Score the clay 'roots' heavily. When the clay is dry, lightly spray with silver paint.

Note: This could be a spring, summer or autumn tree, with the addition of tissue paper blossom, green tissue leaves or gold tissue leaves.

Wire Fish

Before starting this project teach the children how to use a wire cutter and pliers for tightening joins. For younger children, alternative methods are suggested below.

Skeleton fish: Use a piece of florist's wire for the backbone. Thread on beads between 'ribs' of bendy wire which must be wound tightly onto the spine. Younger children could use garden ties, pipe-cleaners or card strips for the ribs. Cut out a card head and tail, and tape them to the backbone. Cover the card with glued fabric oddments and decorate with glittery bits.

Oval fish: Join two pieces of florist's wire at the mouth of the fish. Cross them over and twist them to make the tail. Attach strips of wire inside the frame, tightening the ends with pliers. These wire strips can be curled round a pencil, zig-zagged or threaded through beads, buttons, lace or sequin waste. Younger children could glue or staple lace and Cellophane inside the fish frame.

Plaster

Simple Casting

Sweets

This is an easy project for very young children.

Mix up the plaster, following the instructions on page 71. Put a few teaspoonfuls of mixed plaster into each depression in a plastic tray from a box of chocolates. Turn out the shapes when the plaster is set, then brightly paint or spray with gold paint. The sweets make a popular addition to the class shop or café.

Collections

Impressions can be made in thick slabs of clay by pressing in a collection of shells, pebbles, fossils, coins or handprints.

Prepare the plaster and spoon it carefully into each impression. Leave for several hours and peel off the clay. The clay can be cleaned and used again. Wash the plaster shells in cold water, then dry and paint with muted pinks, blues and browns. Use sponges or stippling brushes for a soft effect. Mount on strong card with PVA glue, and label.

40

Casting Eggs for Easter

Collect the plastic packaging found inside Easter egg boxes to use as moulds. Arrange the moulds inside bowls or dishes so that they will not tip over when filled with plaster. Mix up the plaster (see page 71), and pour some into each mould, making sure that the top is level. When the plaster is set turn the eggs out of the moulds and leave them on a wire rack. Allow them to dry out completely before decorating.

Try some of the following techniques for decoration:

- Sponge-print with two or three watercolours as shown above on the egg in the nest, the bow-tied egg and the blue lace-trimmed egg.

- Spray with gold paint (for moulds with a relief pattern on them).

- Make patterns with felt-tip pens.

- Make a face by sponge-printing and gluing on decorative oddments.

- Create a collage over the surface with cut pieces of bright wrapping paper.

Easter Egg Cards

Use 5-centimetre plastic egg-moulds to cast shapes for chicks, rabbits or Humpty Dumpty. Sponge-print in soft colours when dry and glue onto a stand-up card background.

Note: Two half-eggs can be glued together if the surfaces are flat. Half-eggs make good paperweights for Easter gifts – write a message on card glued to the back. This makes a refreshing alternative to the standard Easter card.

41

Etching in Plaster Slabs

Cast slabs of plaster, 1.5 centimetres thick, in polystyrene trays (see page 71). Turn them out when set and dry off for several days in a warm place. Put on plenty of colour by sponge-printing or spray them gold. When the paint is dry, scratch out your chosen design with a pointed clay tool, and mount on stiff card for added strength.

Note: Try story sequencing on four slabs, with each etching telling a part of the story.

Plaster City

Glue five or six small boxes inside a shoebox onto the base. Ensure each box is securely closed with tape, so that the plaster cannot run into the boxes through the flaps. Fill the shoebox with mixed plaster, to cover the small boxes. When the plaster is totally dry, turn over the whole thing and peel off and discard the shoebox and small boxes. Glue paper doors and windows to the buildings, or draw them with felt-tip pens.

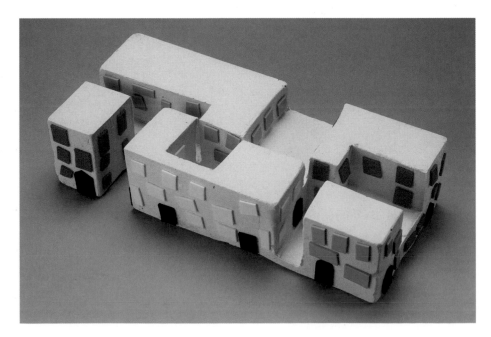

Casting on a Clay Slab

Many items can be impressed onto a slab of clay to give a reverse relief effect when cast in plaster. Try a collection of autumn leaves, seeds and nuts, a collection of seaweeds, a geometric pattern, an insect made by impressing oddments such as screws, washers, sticks and poppy-seed heads, or the contents of a lunch box.

Shown above are:

- A variety of thicknesses of rope and string, pressed into the clay.

- A plastic mother and baby giraffe.

- A drawing scratched into the clay, depicting a familiar poem such as 'The Owl and the Pussycat' by Edward Lear (Corgi, 1997).

- A fish drawn on the clay, with the centre hollowed out using a clay tool with a wire loop.

Roll a slab of clay 2 centimetres thick. Lay your chosen container (polystyrene or plastic tray) on top of the clay and carefully cut around the container. Lay the cut slab of clay inside the container, smoothing the edges against the sides. Now impress any items you wish on to the clay. Pour mixed plaster over the clay impressions to a depth of about 1.5 centimetres. When this has set turn it out carefully, peel off the clay and wash the plaster cast in cold water. Allow it to dry completely before finishing.

Two of the casts above were painted on a sponge-printed background. The rope cast was sprayed gold. The giraffe cast was brushed with brown shoe polish, and then the spots were scratched out with a cocktail stick.

Other finishes to try:

- Paint with matt black paint, particularly filling the crevices. Rub the paint off the high spots before it dries, so that the depressions are darker.

- Paint with a base coat such as blue. Touch the high spots with gold paint using a stippling brush or sponge.

- Give it a shiny coat of diluted PVA glue to highlight the relief effect.

Note: An alternative method of casting a clay slab is to make either a paper collar or a rim of clay. Pour the wet plaster inside and allow it to dry.

Plasterwork Gifts

Hanging Plaque

Roll out a slab of clay to fit a polystyrene tray, as on page 43. Push assorted oddments into the clay to make a picture of, for example, 'mum'. Use plastic construction kit pieces (such as wheels and strips), bricks and plastic lids, screws, bolts, sticks or anything else available. Write the word 'mum' underneath – fortunately, this word is a palindrome, so it does not need to be reversed.

If you want to hang up the plaster cast make two holes at this stage by pushing two pencils or sticks into the clay, standing them upright. Now pour in the mixed plaster (see page 71) and allow it to set completely before removing it from the tray and peeling off the clay. Finish the cast as desired (for ideas, see page 43).

Flower in a Pot

Begin by making the flower. Cut 5 centimetres off the base of a plastic drinks bottle for the flower-shape mould. For the stem, rest a piece of twig or rigid electrical wire in the plastic mould. Mix up the plaster as on page 71, and pour it into the mould, ensuring the bottom of the stem is submerged.

Take a plastic flowerpot and cover the drainage holes at the bottom with tape. When the plaster flower-shape is completely dry, remove the mould and stand the stem upright in the plastic flowerpot. Mix up some more plaster and pour it into the flowerpot, keeping the flower stem centred (if necessary hold it in place with tape).

When the plaster has set, turn out the flower which is now standing in its own plaster pot. Decorate with sponge-painting in two colours, or felt-tip pens, collage, sequins or whatever you wish. Write a message to the recipient of the gift on cut-out card 'leaves'.

Casting with Plaster Bandages

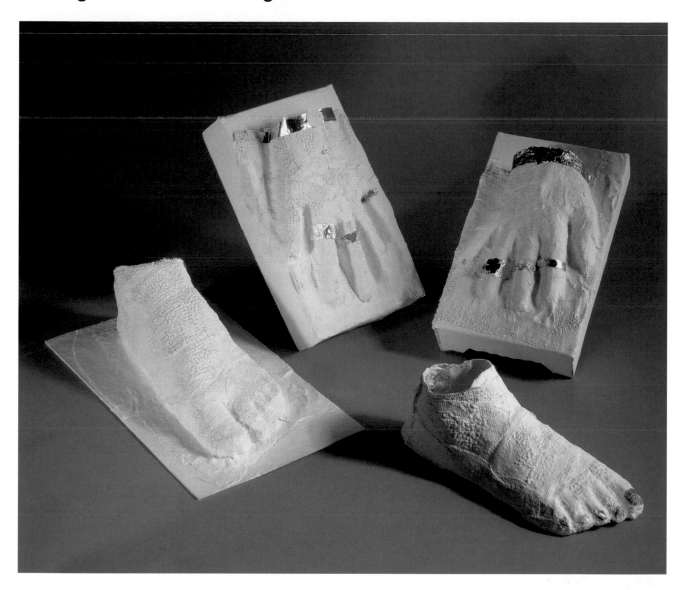

Casting body parts in plaster bandages is great fun. If the children work in pairs, they can take it in turns to make a cast of their partner's hand or foot, while their partner concentrates on being very still.

Prepare everything you need before you start. Protect surfaces with newspaper and fill a shallow dish with water. With dry hands cut up the bandages into 5- and 10-centimetre strips and put the strips in a dry box. Briefly dip each piece of bandage into the water, holding it as flat as possible to avoid creasing, and then apply it to the hand or foot.

The hand or foot to be covered should be rested on a piece of strong card. Cover the hand or foot with overlapping strips of dipped bandage, placing the strips over the flesh and onto the card. Smooth carefully around the fingers and toes. Build up about four or five layers and smooth well. When the plaster is starting to set an adult can cut carefully down the back of the heel or hand, using round-edged scissors. Gently slide out the hand or foot and cover the cut with two strips of dipped bandage to regain the correct shape.

When the cast is completely dry, it can be decorated with rings or nail polish, or painted. If desired, the plaster cast can be gently removed from its card backing and the edges can be trimmed with scissors.

Note: Dipped plaster bandages can be layered over a mould such as a bowl. A plaster cast can also be taken of a face – close adult supervision is essential for this, to ensure no plaster enters the eyes, nose or mouth. A piece of chiffon, with holes cut for the eyes and nose, should be laid over the face before layering the bandage strips, so that the cast can be easily removed. Exciting masks can be made by decorating face casts with paint, feathers, fur and fabric.

Weaving

Cellophane Window Weaving

Make looms from scrap materials, with spaces for strips of Cellophane and crêpe paper in primary colours to be woven in and out.

Round loom: Cut off either the top third or bottom third of a clear plastic bottle. Cut snips all around the bottle, about 2 centimetres wide, leaving the centre piece intact. Fold back each flap to make a flat, wheel-shaped loom (see diagram below).

Round loom

Weave paper strips around the centre, mixing Cellophane and tissue. Tie or staple the ends of the strips together and add decorative knots or Cellophane oddments.

Rectangular loom: Waste-paper packaging with a pattern of holes in it can be used for a rectangular loom, but an alternative can be made by folding and cutting a piece of A4 card (see diagram, right). Stretch it out and take the coloured strips for a walk through the spaces, vertically, horizontally, diagonally, or at random. Interesting effects occur as primary colours overlap.

Rectangular loom

Bottle loom: Cut off and reserve the bottom 4 centimetres of a clear plastic bottle. Now cut long snips all the way up the bottle from the bottom almost to the top. Tape all the bottom cut edges back together again (an adult will need to do this), creating spaces for weaving 'in the round' (see diagram, right).

Bottle loom

The children will enjoy experimenting with tying knots in the ends, making plaits and twists, and taping on tassels and streamers. When the bottle is covered with weaving, push the cut-off bottle-end back into the base (reversed), to retain a good rounded shape.

Note: Direct sunlight will fade crêpe paper.

Twig Weaving

Natural Materials

For the twig weaving shown left, choose a strong twig with a single fork. Stretch rubber bands evenly across the fork to form the warp. Weave in and out of the bands any natural materials you have, such as grasses, barley, dried flower-heads, feathers or strips of bark.

Winter is a good time to collect dead heads such as *sedum* and *hydrangea*, or coloured twigs such as *cornus*. Short-lived spring weaving could include catkins, pussy willow and bursting buds. Late summer is a good collecting time for clematis, poppy and cornflower seed-heads, grasses and cereals.

Plastic Materials

Whole class project

The large double-forked branch shown below can be used for a whole class project.

The loom will need to be prepared by an adult to ensure the warp threads do not move about:

- either cut small notches with a hacksaw every 2–3 centimetres along the outer edges of the branch

- or knock in a row of nails or drawing pins.

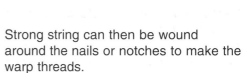

Strong string can then be wound around the nails or notches to make the warp threads.

Ask each child to contribute an item made of plastic to weave into the threads. Use plastic bags, cut-up detergent bottles, plastic string and wire and bubble-wrap strips to make the framework. Small items such as a comb, toothbrush, knife and fork, plastic glove and coat-hanger can then be threaded in.

Note: Other collections to try could include metals, fabrics or papers.

47

Woven Baskets and Pots

Blue and Purple Baskets

Use a flowerpot for a loom. Wind strong thread through the holes in the bottom and round the rim. The small basket uses a 5-centimetre flowerpot, which has eight holes (giving eight warp threads). The large basket uses a 9-centimetre pot: these usually only have six holes in the base so use a nail to punch six more holes in the base. This will give twelve holes for twelve warp threads.

Weave ribbons, wool or fabric strips around the pot, in and out of the warp threads. Glue down the ends and add a handle.

Yellow Basket

This is made with a flat strip of weaving curved into a tube.

Make a loom measuring 30 x 9 centimetres from card, with 1-centimetre snips along the long edges, 2 centimetres apart (see diagram below).

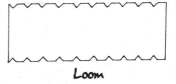

Loom

Wind thread around the notches for the warp. Weave fabric strips from side to side, trim the edges and staple the two sides of the woven card together. Bend the woven card into a square, circular or oval shape. Make a fold 1 centimetre from the bottom of the notched card, and glue it to a corresponding shaped card base. Neaten the top edge by gluing on a strip of felt.

Pussy Willow Pot

Cut the bottom 12 centimetres off a plastic drinks bottle and wrap several rows of double-sided sticky tape around it. Cut 14-centimetre lengths of pussy willow twigs or hay stalks and press them around the bottle and secure with two rubber bands.

Tie a ball of wool to a twig and weave four or five rows of wool in and out of the twigs near the top and again near the bottom. The weaving will hold the twigs securely and the rubber bands can then be removed. Younger children may wish to omit the weaving and tie ribbons round instead.

Note: Red and yellow *cornus* twigs also make an attractive pot.

Clay on a Woven Background

For the clay items, roll and cut out a selection of small slabs on your chosen theme, such as 'The sea' (shown above). Make two holes through each clay slab, so they can be attached to the background. Dry the clay pieces and then spray with silver paint, or they can be fired and glazed.

To make the loom, you need an old picture frame. It is possible to tie the warp threads straight onto the frame, although they are likely to move about. For much easier weaving, it is worth taking the time to ensure that the warp threads are fixed. Tap in a row of drawing pins along the top and bottom edges of the back of the frame. Tie the warp threads (green string was used above) onto the pins from top to bottom. Your loom is now ready for weaving. If you do not have a picture frame use a very thick piece of card notched along the top and bottom edges to take the warp threads.

Now tear up lots of strips of fabric for the weft (try chiffon, silk, cotton, nets, ribbons and thick wools, in a mix of appropriate colours). Weave these from one side of the frame to the other, pushing down each row to create a springy background. Knots may be tied in fabric strips for extra texture and ragged edges of cloth will look more interesting than cut edges. Trim the side edges, and add a touch of glue here and there to keep the 'waves' in place. Finally, tie in the clay pieces. Thread silver yarn through the holes and tie at the back of the work. Further decoration, including stitching, can be added if desired.

Seasonal Fabric Weaving

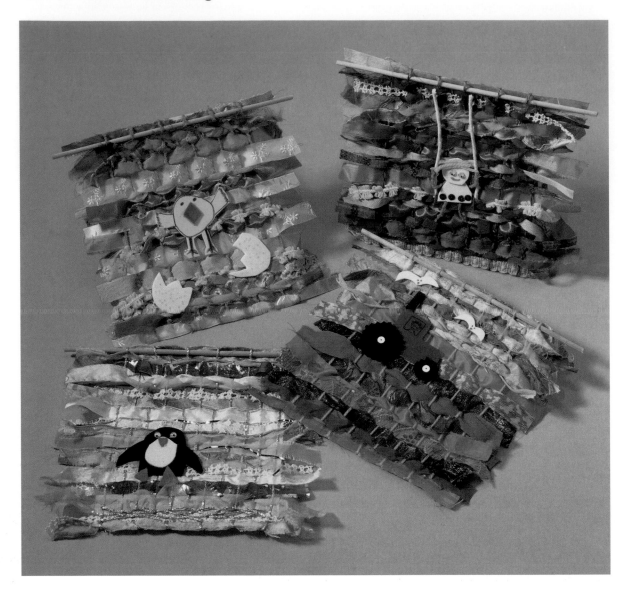

Use a commercial card loom sized about 15 x 20 centimetres. Wind up the warp threads for younger children, but allow older children to do it themselves. Use pink wool for spring, green for summer, yellow for autumn and silver for winter.

The colours used above are

- **Spring:** soft greens and yellows, with bits of flowered ribbon

- **Summer:** vibrant greens and blues

- **Autumn:** russets and gold

- **Winter:** soft blues, silvers and white lace.

Tear up fabric strips into 25-centimetre lengths for the weft, choosing colours appropriate for each season. Allow the children to select their own colours. Weave the strips straight across from one side to the other, leaving the ends loose.

Push the rows of weaving together to achieve a good texture. When the loom is covered with weaving, cut the warp threads at the back and remove the loom. Glue on a piece of card or fabric to stabilise the weaving. The warp threads can be taped to the back or tied together in pairs.

Finish the work by gluing or stitching on an appropriate seasonal item cut from coloured felt, for example, a tractor for autumn. Add any other decorative items or stitches to complete the work.

Chain-link Fence Sunrise

Collect lots of plastic bags or old raincoats in reds, oranges and yellows. Cut these into long strips about 3 centimetres wide and add strips of plastic ribbon, wire and vegetable netting.

Weave the strips in and out of the fence, starting at the bottom centre and adding curved rows close together, to create a large sunrise. Put in plenty of staples when starting rows or joining strips. Add some 'rays of sunshine' in yellow and gold strips.

Note: Fence weaving is adaptable – try the school logo, or a seaside or winter theme. Animal or boat outlines can be cut from plastic and stapled on to the woven background.

Weaving in Sequin Waste

A tin covered with weaving or a woven bag make useful gifts.

Cut an oblong of sequin waste. Weave rows of coloured wools or torn fabric strips across the waste. Every alternate row of holes should be sufficient. Leave the ends loose at the sides or trim them.

Either glue your weaving around a tin, or fold it in half and glue or stitch the sides together to make a bag.

Note: Weaving sequin waste is also effective for bookmarks, little mats and card decoration.

Weaving inside an Outline

For these woven pictures, you need a small polystyrene tray and a selection of wools. Keep the picture fairly small, as wool weaving takes some time.

To make the warp:
Draw a simple pencil outline (circle, oval, triangle or oblong) on a polystyrene tray. Prick holes around the outline with a needle. Sew in the warp threads with wool across the outline (vertical warp for the face, robin and house, and horizontal warp for the tree).

To make the weft:
Thread a curved bodkin with wool and weave it in and out of the warp threads, turning at the end of each row, until the outline is covered. Tuck loose ends and joins behind the weaving. Join areas of different colours together, so that there are no gaps in the work. Keep the edges loose, without pulling the weft too tightly, to maintain a good outline. Pack the rows together for a good texture and colour. 'Hair' can be made with loose, looped stitches, made randomly in and out of the warp.

Further decorative details, such as felt, buttons or sequins, can be glued to the finished work. Trim the tray with an edging of whipped running stitches, sewn into holes pricked at 1-centimetre intervals.

Note: Instead of using a polystyrene tray, the warp threads can be stitched onto a paper plate or piece of card.

Wool Weaving

The weavings shown above can be made on card looms cut with notches for the warp threads. Weave wool in and out of the warp using a curved bodkin (or a plastic drinks stirrer with a hole in one end).

Long weaving: Wind up ten warp threads on a long rectangular loom. Weave in short lengths of natural coloured wools, turning after each row and leaving any new ends at the sides. When the weaving is complete, cut the warp threads and tie them in pairs, or tie to a piece of cane. Tuck the side ends into the back of the work and decorate with dried flowers or grasses.

Tree weaving: Draw a tree outline on paper, using a black felt-tip pen, and tape this behind the warp threads of your loom. Cover the outline with rows of weaving in green and brown wools, carefully following the drawing underneath the warp. Leave the ends at the sides and cut them off later for a shaggy outline. Alternatively, the ends can be woven into the work or taped to the back. Glue the tree to thin card to stabilise the weaving and add red felt apples. Outline weavings can be sewn or glued to collage work to add extra texture.

Sheep weaving: Proceed as for the tree, covering a sheep outline drawing with weaving. Build up the rows, turning at the edges and taking care not to pull the wool too tightly. Tuck stray ends behind the weaving. Next, weave the background in blue and green wools, joining it carefully to the sheep so that no holes appear in the work. Cut the warp threads and tie them in pairs with a cane at the top. Tape the side ends to the back. Add extra details, such as legs and a head using black felt.

Ship weaving: Use a ship outline, as for the sheep, but do not join the background to the outline. Instead, pass the needle behind the ship on each row and work to the other side. Experiment with twisted and plaited threads for a rich texture. Add felt detail, if desired.

Weaving in Netting

You will need a piece of strong plastic netting, such as a fruit bag or garden net, and a collection of dried grasses, straw, wools, twigs, cereals and flower seed-heads (such as poppy, clematis and corn cockle).

Thread a piece of cane through the top of the net. Then weave in a row of grasses and flowerheads, threading them vertically. Next, weave several rows, working from side to side, under the grasses. Use various thicknesses of wool through a bodkin or a bunch of straw stems. If you put a piece of tape over the end of a bunch of straw stems, it can be threaded easily through the net.

The weaving does not have to be exact – any holes can be used. Continue to add alternating rows of grasses (vertically) and weaving (horizontally) until the net is covered. Trim off unwanted ends.

Note: Instead of working in rows a much freer weaving can be made by working in any direction, for example, diagonals, zig-zags or circles.

Warp Variations

The colour of the warp threads can be varied to make striped weaves, for example, four white threads, four black threads, four white threads, and so on.

The woven mat on the left uses torn strips of soft fabric (pink and mauve warp, with purple and white weaving). The mat on the right is worked in wool (white and black for the warp, with white and blue weaving).

Use a separate piece of wool or fabric for each row of weaving, leaving the ends at the sides. Tie the weft ends in pairs, then the warp ends, and trim off the ends.

Fabric

Creative Stitching using Felt

Spring Flowers

You will need coloured felt and oddments of lace, braid, beads and buttons.

For the background cut out a circle of neutral fabric (approximately 25 centimetres in diameter). Cut a variety of flower shapes and a butterfly from coloured felt. Arrange and pin these onto the background, leaving 2 centimetres clear round the edge of the circle. Stitch the flowers in place using a running stitch or cross stitch. Embellish with scraps of lace, and braid stems, beads or buttons for flower centres.

To pad the work glue a circle of wadding (20 centimetres in diameter) onto a piece of card, apply glue to the card all around the wadding, and press the stitching down around the wadding. Finally, cut a circular window (22 centimetres in diameter) out of a piece of brightly coloured card, and glue the card over the stitching to frame it. Attach a piece of ribbon for hanging.

Musical Instruments

Ask the children to practise sketching their chosen instrument from observation before beginning the stitching.

Draw the shape of the instrument on coloured felt and cut it out. Pin and stitch it onto a piece of hessian or open-weave fabric. Stitch on patterns, buttons, beads or other appropriate details.

Fray the edges of the hessian and mount the sewing on card or cloth.

Fabric Collage

The cat and rabbit fabric collage pictures shown above are glued onto a plain fabric background. The pirate and witch collage pictures are appliquéd onto a glued fabric background.

Cat and rabbit pictures: Begin by drawing an outline of an animal on paper, then transfer it lightly onto a piece of background fabric. Fill in the animal outline with glued oddments of material, for example, browns for the rabbit, black and whites for the cat. Glue on any other details you wish, such as string whiskers and a rug for the cat, or a wool outline and a field for the rabbit. Finish with sequins, lace, ribbon, beads, braid or a little stitching.

Pirate and witch pictures: Make the background first. Choose a piece of appropriately coloured cloth of the correct size. Cut more strips of cloth, making the edges rough and wavy, and lay these over the back cloth, horizontally. Chiffon and sheers work well as they allow other colours to show through. When you are satisfied with the fabric overlays, either stitch them down or glue very lightly.

Next, draw an outline of your chosen subject on paper, and work out the pieces of fabric you need to cut out. Cut and pin the pieces to the background and stitch them in place. Glue on any other details you wish, or embellish with a little fabric paint.

Note: Make the borders from four strips of card wrapped in wools (see page 35). Choose two colours only to tone with the picture.

Batik Cushions

First you will need to prepare

- pieces of white cotton cloth 40 centimetres square

- wax melted in a wax pot, and a brush

- ready-mixed coloured dyes.

Start by sketching the cushion design on paper. When you are ready to begin lay a square of cotton on some kitchen paper and paint the design onto the cloth with a brush dipped in melted wax. Next, paint all the spaces with brightly coloured dyes.

When the work is dry, iron it between several changes of newspaper to remove the wax. Make up into a cushion cover.

Note: Supervise children using hot wax and protect clothing from dyes.

Display Cloth

Group project

Plan the display cloth layout together as a group or class and draw the animal outlines in pencil on the cloth. Apply wax to the outlines and then paint the animals and the background with brightly coloured dyes. When the wax has been removed by ironing the cloth between several changes of newspaper, add black fabric paint to the animal outlines to emphasise details.

This colourful batik on African animals can be used as a display cloth. Large pieces such as this can also be made into a roller blind or curtain for windows or shelving. Alternatively, use it as a hanging to improve an unattractive spot.

Edible Patchwork

Whole class project

This is great fun to make because the children can sample some of the ingredients during the process.

Begin by collecting an interesting range of food items that will not go mouldy or soggy. Cut pieces of felt, about 12 centimetres square, in two contrasting colours. Each child can plan their work on equivalent-sized paper first, by arranging their chosen food items and drawing in the stitches they want to add.

Stitch or glue the food items to the squares of felt. Some children will attempt quite complicated patterns, faces or figures. Many items can be pierced with a needle, although some will need stitches over them to keep them in place. Other items can be glued onto a felt square, with a little decorative stitching around them.

Items shown above include:

- stitched soft sweets such as dolly mixtures, marshmallows and liquorice. Circular mints with holes are easy to sew on. Avoid very sticky sweets

- stitched pasta such as penne, radiatori and taped spaghetti bundles

- glued dried foods such as kidney beans, butter beans and peppercorns. Melon seeds and raisins are threaded on strings. Poppadoms are glued and stitched

- various other stitched items include a sprig of rosemary, tea bags, bay leaves, onion skins, lollipops and crisps with holes.

Other items to try are peanuts, wrapped sweets, dried chillies, star anise, apple rings, biscuits, pasta with holes or bunches of herbs.

Finally, glue all the squares onto a strong backing and glue on a felt border.

Note: Collaborative patchwork, one square per child, is useful for displaying collections such as plastics, shiny things, round objects or textured items.

Feltwork Sampler

Group project

This large collaborative piece uses 21 squares of blue felt and 21 squares of white, each 15 centimetres square. It incorporates collage, appliqué, weaving and raised feltwork.

Begin by cutting out felt letters to make the name of the school. Then stitch on dolly mixtures and circular mints with holes. Buttons, beads or other oddments can be substituted for sweets. Appliqué each letter onto a felt square and stitch on a border of sequin waste.

Make looms in dark felt for weaving. Fold and cut the felt as shown in the diagram, right. Weave strips of fabric (in blues, greys and purples) in and out of the spaces in the loom, and trim the edges. Decorate white squares with glued-on oddments of blue felt cut into triangles, strips and semicircles. Create a textured, raised effect by knotting, plaiting, rolling, twisting, looping, curling, gathering or tying bows.

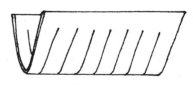

Felt loom

Arrange all the completed squares on a large piece of cotton backing, and glue them in place. Older children may wish to stitch on the squares, or quilt the work by stitching in a layer of wadding. Glue or stitch on long strips of felt for the borders. Decorate the border with felt collage work of children playing, adding any other stitching or details you wish.

Stitching with Nets

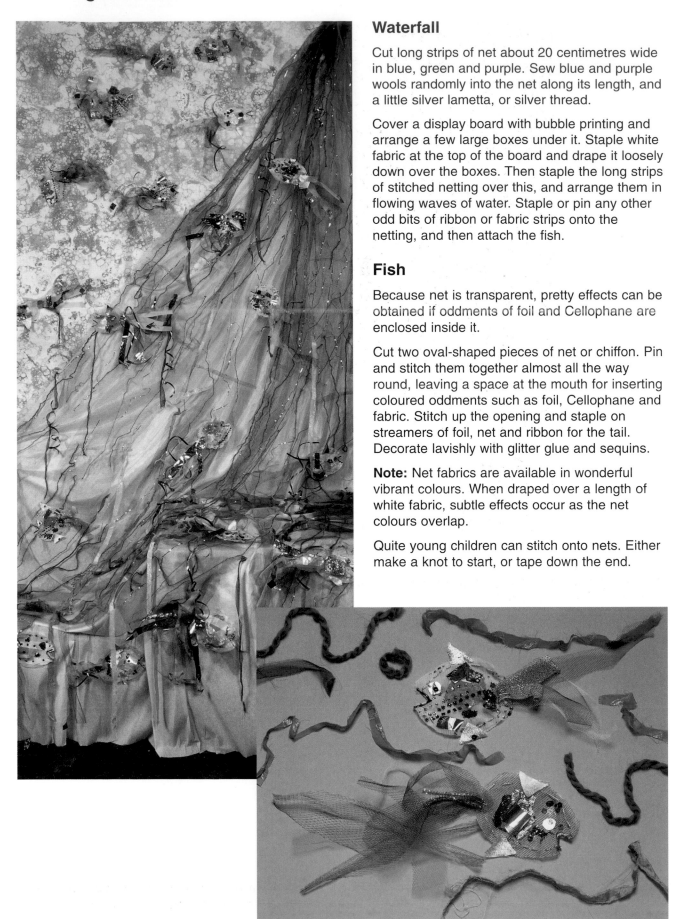

Waterfall

Cut long strips of net about 20 centimetres wide in blue, green and purple. Sew blue and purple wools randomly into the net along its length, and a little silver lametta, or silver thread.

Cover a display board with bubble printing and arrange a few large boxes under it. Staple white fabric at the top of the board and drape it loosely down over the boxes. Then staple the long strips of stitched netting over this, and arrange them in flowing waves of water. Staple or pin any other odd bits of ribbon or fabric strips onto the netting, and then attach the fish.

Fish

Because net is transparent, pretty effects can be obtained if oddments of foil and Cellophane are enclosed inside it.

Cut two oval-shaped pieces of net or chiffon. Pin and stitch them together almost all the way round, leaving a space at the mouth for inserting coloured oddments such as foil, Cellophane and fabric. Stitch up the opening and staple on streamers of foil, net and ribbon for the tail. Decorate lavishly with glitter glue and sequins.

Note: Net fabrics are available in wonderful vibrant colours. When draped over a length of white fabric, subtle effects occur as the net colours overlap.

Quite young children can stitch onto nets. Either make a knot to start, or tape down the end.

Rainbow Collage Hanging

Group project

This is a group project for approximately ten children, with each child contributing one decorated fabric strip in all the seven rainbow colours.

Cut or tear ten strips of fabric in red, orange, yellow, green, blue, indigo and violet. Different colour tones and patterned fabrics will add to the richness of the final piece. Collect scrap items that can be stitched, glued, tied, taped or stapled onto the fabric strips. Younger children could glue and staple, whereas older children could use a mixture of techniques.

Techniques shown above include:

- pink fabric strips, tied on in bows
- purple strips cut from plastic bags, tied on
- blue pieces of polystyrene, glued on
- green knots cut from thick fishing net, tied on with green wool
- yellow Cellophane squares, stapled on
- orange circles cut from plastic bags, stitched on like buttons
- red vegetable netting strips, stapled onto red fabric.

Glue one end of each decorated strip around half an old hoop and decorate it further if required with lametta, felt or sequins. Strips of felt in each of the seven colours can be glued along the hoop to hold the work securely together.

Stiffened Fabric

Fabric Pots

Fabric can be stiffened by brushing it with a good coating of diluted PVA glue. For a mould use a plastic bottle or pot covered with cling film. Drape the glued fabric over the upturned pot and arrange the folds carefully. Add any other details while the glue is wet.

Shown left are:

- glitter on a circle of patterned fabric
- tissue paper pieces over a square of yellow fabric
- a square of lace over a square of purple cotton.

When the glue is dry and hard remove the stiffened fabric pot from the mould.

Fabric Face and Hat

For the face: Arrange two apples, a pear and a banana on a plastic tray to resemble a face. Carefully cover them with a layer of cling film and drape pieces of glued cloth over the fruit, smoothing them into the crevices. When the glue is quite dry, remove the stiff face, trim the edges and decorate it by adding hair, eye and mouth details. Glue the face onto a stick to make a puppet.

For the hat: Cut and glue a large circle of fabric. Drape it over a bowl (covered with cling film) which fits the head. Leave it to dry on a flat plastic surface. The fabric should overlap the bowl and lie flat on the plastic surface. When the hat is dry, remove the bowl, trim the edges around the rim and decorate with ribbons, tissue paper, foils and feathers.

Paper and Wood

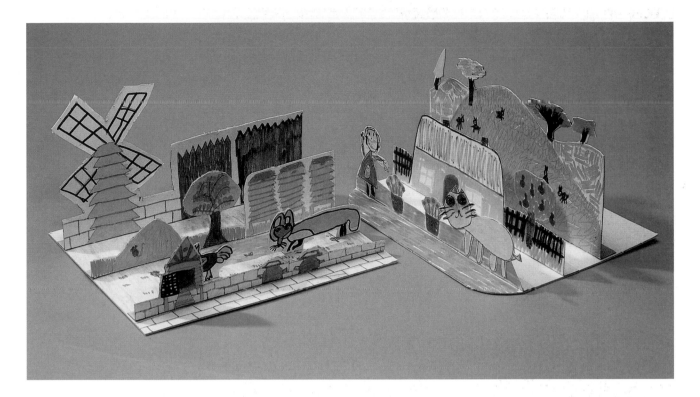

Card Landscapes

House and garden scene: The landscape above right has three stand-up card layers (12, 9 and 6 centimetres high); the bottom edges have been folded under by 1.5 centimetres.

Discuss with the children the difference in size between near objects (such as themselves or the playground), middle distance objects (such as a house or road) and far away things (such as a hill or church spire). Then ask the children to draw a scene on the three cards to represent each distance, and cut them out. Glue the 1.5-centimetre folded edges of each scene to a baseboard in the appropriate height order.

Windmill scene: The landscape above left, drawn by an older child, shows a journey from a story (*Rosie's Walk* by Pat Hutchins, Bodley Head, 1998). The three layers need to be carefully planned to show all stages of the journey. Draw, cut out and stick down the layers on the baseboard by folding the bottom edges.

Note: Other journeys to try include 'My journey to school', 'The journey of the Magi' and 'A journey through a creepy forest'.

Photographs in a Scene

Put real photographic cut-outs of the children into a scene. The playground scene shown right is entitled 'Playing with My Friend at School'.

Draw items such as a play house, tunnel, ball, pond or hopscotch game onto three layers of card. Cut out and glue them to the baseboard. The two photographed friends were cut out and glued to the foreground.

Note: Photographs of several landscape features can be used, such as a church, tree or house.

Paper Tube Sculpture

Paper or card tubes can be imaginatively cut and assembled. Show the children how to make a tube stand up, by snipping around the base, splaying out the ends, and gluing it to a baseboard. Try cutting a tube into slices, or unravelling it diagonally, or cutting it lengthways into curved strips. Interesting structures can be built by cutting two notches at the end of a tube and pushing another tube into the notches.

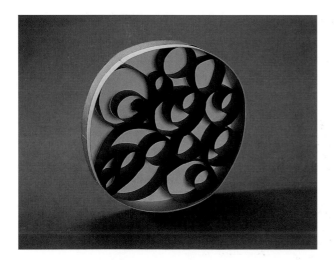

Coils

Cut several paper strips 3 centimetres wide. Use a long strip of card to make a circular frame and make lots of small coils of different sizes with the paper strips. Arrange these creatively within the circular frame. Use a minimal amount of paper glue to keep the coils in place.

Make the structure rigid by gluing card, coloured Cellophane or tissue paper to the back.

Spirals

Use a piece of strong card for the base. Glue on three or four different lengths of wooden dowel or plastic tube for the uprights. Draw spirals on paper circles and cut them out. Decorate the spirals with paint or felt-tip pens and glue them into place.

Happy Birthday Surprise Box

This project can be adapted for any celebration.

Cut out the front of a 1-litre fruit juice carton, leaving a 1-centimetre rim around the front edges. Cover the carton with wrapping paper. Carefully measure and make a frame for the front of the box using four strips of card. Glue the frame to the top and bottom of the box, but do not glue the sides.

Make two card doors just tall enough to slide behind the sides of the frame. Decorate the frame and doors as you wish with a message, drawings and patterns. Slide the doors into place to open and close the box.

Design the inside of the box. Shown above is a birthday cake made from dough. You could put in a real cake, a bag of sweets, standing card figures, a mobile or model.

Imaginative Paper Landscape

To create the 'adventure playground' shown left, experiment with making slides, tunnels, climbing frames and roundabouts cut out of paper.

Show the children a variety of paper techniques:

- fold paper strips into triangles
- coil strips or make paper chains
- fold in zig-zags, as fans or steps
- make curls and spirals
- cut streamers and fringes.

Other paper landscapes to try include a rainforest, park, swamp, volcano, underwater scene, secret garden or crazy flower garden.

Paper Sculpture: Cutting and Folding

Demonstrate ways to fold a square:

A – edge to edge, into oblongs or squares

B – diagonally, into triangles

C – zig-zag folds, into four (or more) strips.

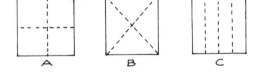

Cut lots of 10-centimetre squares of scrap paper so that the children can practise folding and cutting.

Show the children a variety of cutting options (see below) and encourage them to experiment with designs. Choose their best designs for copying onto squares of brightly coloured paper.

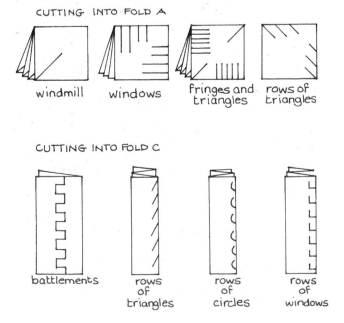

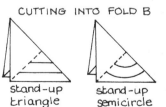

Carefully open out the cut papers and fold out the cut sections. Mount on a card backing sheet with hole-punched borders.

Note: The children may like to try a combination of cuts such as windows with stand-up triangles, or a stand-up triangle on a fold A instead of a fold B. Extra hole patterns can be added to each design using a hole punch.

Outdoor Mural in Wood

Group project

Collect a good assortment of wood offcuts in various shapes and colours. Very small oddments are useful for eyes, leaves or tails, and tiny scraps of balsa, matchsticks or lollysticks can be used, along with branched twigs, pine cones, round wheels and bark chippings.

Brainstorm with the children and make a list of what could be included in a wooden outdoor scene. They can then sketch out ideas from which the mural can be planned.

On a large piece of marine board, pencil in the main background features, such as fields, hills, rivers and roads. Apply wood dyes to show the skyline, the road, ripples on the river and ploughed lines on the fields. Remember to protect children's clothes.

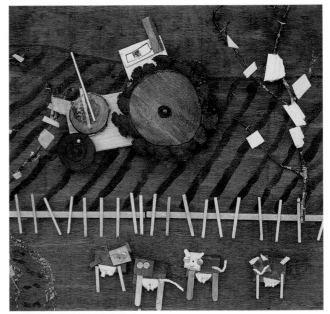

Groups of children can then make all the items they want to include using wood pieces. Shown here are houses, vehicles, people, trees, hedges and fences, a church (with inscribed tombstones), animals and tractors in fields and a village school's duck race on the river. Use wood glue and nails to join wood together.

When all the individual pieces are dry, arrange them on the background and glue or nail them in place. If the mural is to be hung outside, coat everything with a layer or two of yacht varnish.

Life-size Wooden Figures

Group project
Observe the variety of body positions demonstrated by children at playtime.

Discuss with the children the various poses that can be seen, such as children sitting, reclining, leaning or hanging. Look at sculptures or photographs for ideas.

Provide an assortment of wood offcuts in a variety of shapes and sizes, and nails, hammers, saws, wire, string, wood-glue and wheels.

Working in groups of three or four, the children need to choose a site for their outdoor sculpture, such as sitting in a tree or on a bench, leaning against a fence, looking into the pond or climbing on a climbing frame.

Make heads, bodies, arms and legs and fix them together with nails, glue and wire. Add extra details, for example, hair and fingers, and perhaps something a figure can hold, such as a cup of tea or radio. Prop, tie or nail the figures in place in their chosen site. Finally, coat with varnish for durability.

Wooden Pets

Use small oddments of balsa wood, bark chips, twigs, offcuts and wood shavings.

No sawing or hammering is involved. The children have to look for pieces of wood with appropriate shapes for the pet they want to make. Glue all the pieces together.

Note: Masking tape is useful for holding pieces together until the glue dries.

Temporary Wood Sculptures

Group project

Collect a large sack of log oddments and offcuts of various sizes. Explain the task: the children are going to create a picture on the playground using the pieces of wood. Shown above is an 'elephant at a water hole' and below is a 'giraffe eating'. Suitable themes might be: African animals, vehicles, buildings, pets, people, toys, fantasy figures or the school logo.

Allow a small group of two or three children to work at a time and change the sculptures every few days. The children will eagerly await their turn and become very enthusiastic as they realise what is required.

Instead of wood offcuts, all kinds of other materials can be used, such as shells, pebbles, building bricks, pieces of flintstones or pine cones. Soft sculptures could utilise leaves, grass and flowers.

A popular activity is to arrange materials around a child lying on the ground, resulting in a life-size outline figure. This can then be 'dressed' by filling in the outline with details for the face and clothes using any materials you wish.

Working with Withies

Withy Lady

You will need some withies soaked in water for a few days, and plaster bandages.

Tie a bunch of withies together about half-way down and make them stand up by spreading them out at the bottom. Separate the bunch into two legs, with a bent withy triangle tied on for each foot, as shown left. An alternative method is to tie in a circle of withy near the ground, making a cone-shaped withy skirt.

Stuff bubble wrap into the body and tie the withies together at the neck. Push another bundle of withies right through the body to make the arms. Curve a withy into a circle for the head and tie it in securely.

Dip pieces of plaster bandage in water and cover or mould whichever parts you wish, adding fingers and facial features. Tie in clothing, jewellery and accessories.

Withy Birds

Bend a soaked withy into a bird shape and join with masking tape. Use small pieces of bent withy to make the beaks, wings and feet, and curl withies into circles for eyes. Tape all the pieces together and glue coloured tissue to the back.

Shapes to try :

butterfly

bird

cat or person

fish

turtle or ladybird

face

animal or duck

Recipes and Rules

Playdough recipe

1. Put into a pan:
   - 200g plain flour
   - 100g salt
   - 2 teaspoons cream of tartar
   - 1 tablespoon of cooking oil
   - 300ml water containing your chosen food colouring
2. Cook and stir well for a few minutes, until the mixture is thick and stiff.
3. Turn out the dough, cool it, and knead well until it is soft and pliable.

Salt dough recipe

1. Mix together until pliable:
   - 300g plain flour
   - 300g salt
   - 1 tablespoon of cooking oil
   - 200ml water (or a little more if necessary)
2. Knead on a floured board until smooth and elastic.
3. Bake small items for 10–20 minutes on an oiled baking tray at 180°C. Leave larger items to cook overnight at 110°C. If the inside is still slightly soft after cooking, leave the work to continue to air dry.

Note: Salt dough expands slightly after baking, so if you want to hang up your work make a good sized hole at the top (or push in a paperclip). Colour can be added in the mixing water, as in the playdough recipe.

Making and Using Slip

1. To make slip, put a few small pieces of clay into a paint pot, add a little water and stir to a creamy consistency.
2. Scratch both surfaces that are to be joined and paint the slip onto them.
3. Gently press the two surfaces together.

Newspaper Pulp Recipe

1. Soak a shredded newspaper overnight in a bucket of hot water.
2. Knead the newspaper to a pulp using your hands, a potato masher, or best of all a liquidiser half-full of water.
3. Sieve and drain extremely well, squeezing out as much water as possible to leave a crumbly pulp.
4. Add half a cup of cellulose paste until it feels like soft clay. (Use PVA glue instead of cellulose for a stronger pulp, or even add some sawdust for strength.)

Mixing Plaster

1. Cover the floor and work surfaces with newspaper sheeting.
2. Fill a bucket with water for washing hands and spoons.
3. Make sure your mould or design is ready as plaster sets in 5 to 15 minutes.
4. Half fill a plastic bowl with water and sprinkle in plaster until it starts to build up above the surface of the water. Keep adding plaster into any empty areas of water, and leave for one minute. As an approximate guide, 3 cups of water need 5 cups of plaster.
5. Stir the plaster vigorously with your hand under water to eliminate lumps and bubbles. Look at your hand as a test: if the skin colour can be seen, the mixture is a little too thin.

Note: Use only plastic bowls or buckets for mixing. Always add plaster to water, never the other way round. Never pour plaster down a sink.

For details of further Belair publications,
please write to Libby Masters,
BELAIR PUBLICATIONS LIMITED,
Apex Business Centre,
Boscombe Road, Dunstable, LU5 4RL.

For sales and distribution in North America and South America,
INCENTIVE PUBLICATIONS,
3835 Cleghorn Avenue, Nashville, Tn 37215,
USA.

For sales and distribution in Australia,
EDUCATIONAL SUPPLIES PTY LTD,
8 Cross Street, Brookvale, NSW 2100,
Australia.

For sales and distribution (in other territories),
FOLENS PUBLISHERS,
Apex Business Centre,
Boscombe Road, Dunstable, LU5 4RL,
United Kingdom.
Email: folens@folens.com